# LEARNING WEALTH

# LEARNING WEALTH

## The A–Z of Loving to Learn

## ROZ TOWNSEND

TOWNSEND EDUCATION & SKILLS

First published 1995 by
Townsend Education & Skills Pty Ltd
P.O. Box 1066, Bathurst, New South Wales, Australia, 2795
Phone/Fax 011 61 63 31 4500
© Roslyn Townsend, 1995
Edited, designed and electronically composed by
Murray Child & Company Pty Ltd, Collaroy, NSW
Printed in Canada by Friesens Corporation, Book Division,
Altona, Manitoba


Townsend, Roz.
Learning Wealth: the A–Z of loving to learn.

Bibliography.
ISBN 0 646 23147 2.

1. Learning. 2. Motivation in education. I. Title.

370.154

# ACKNOWLEDGEMENTS

For the development and production of this book I feel a deep sense of gratitude to:

–Iain—my best friend, partner and husband—for his overwhelming support and encouragement. His belief and shared vision for *Learning Wealth* have brought the idea of the book to reality.

–my wonderfully patient children, Zoë and Bella.

–my sister Dottie, for her constant love, interest and support.

–the beautiful memory of my mother, Hazel Hughes, who encouraged my love of learning.

–the memory of my father, who taught me the value of perseverance.

–Jack Collis for his sound advice.

–Margaret McAlister for her inspirational editing.

–Vince O'Farrell for his wickedly humorous illustrations.

–Chris Unsworth for her help in the shorthand section.

–my dear friends and colleagues for their faith in this book.

# CONTENTS

# INTRODUCTION

In today's competitive business environment it is essential you develop speedy and effective ways of accessing and retaining information. People who have these new skills perform better in their workplace, gain more promotions and contracts and have higher self-esteem. It's for this reason that I have called this book *Learning Wealth*.

The ideas are simple and effective. You will find that learning can be easy and fun. Its benefits are available to you even if you did poorly at school.

Students, business professionals, managers, new recruits working their way up and people being retrained discover that learning is a lifelong process. So how can you make it as simple and effective as possible?

The methods I give:

- are fun
- are simple
- save you time
- work for everyone
- can be incorporated into your daily life

**If you keep doing what you've always done you'll keep getting what you've always got.** So be ready for some changes in the way you view yourself and your abilities. But you must be prepared to do some things a little differently!

To help you make the changes that really matter in your life I will be challenging you to take the first small steps. In each chapter you will be given challenges but you really need to treat these as commands. Why? Because most of what we read, novels and so on, encourage us to be passive rather than active. We have to break this pattern and move out of our comfort zone.

Stepping out of our old ways of doing things is a bit like spring cleaning or, as I discovered, like renovating houses! In our early married life my husband and I were short of money and so we renovated a couple of houses. I usually ended up doing the painting. I was painting away happily one day humming to myself when an old friend of ours called in to see how we were doing. He stood at the bottom of the ladder and gazed around. I could tell from the expression on his face that there was something he wanted to say.
'All right,' I said putting down my paint brush. 'Out with it. What am I doing wrong?'
He laughed. 'Am I that obvious? Well...' He hesitated. 'I know you're new to this, but the paint job will last a lot longer if you clean away the old peeling paint, cobwebs and dirt before starting.'

The same applies to learning. If you prepare your mind and

body by clearing away the old ideas which you have about how you learn, the chances are the new you will learn faster, retain more and be far more successful.

**So this book is about preparing your mind and body for learning.**

Most of the ideas I'm presenting have been around for a long while. I didn't invent them, but I have been using them successfully with nearly four thousand students over six years. Oh, and I've used them in my own life to start a business, raise a family, complete a Master's Degree and to help juggle the competing demands of modern life. So I think I can confidently tell you: 'They work!'

This book will springboard you into action. I've included references so you can follow up the ideas that have the most appeal to you.

'Well Roz,' you might ask, 'if these ideas have been around for so long, why aren't more people using them?' The answer is simple: the incredible amount of information to be learnt by both teachers and students has been so demanding that there has been little time left for the process of learning to learn. It's not the fault of the teachers—I know: I taught in our school system for a number of years, and I realised that teachers in our education system are doing a great job with the limited resources and training that the government is able to provide. So here you are —the simple, effective secrets of *Learning Wealth* are right here in this book.

# The Philosophy

Your brain has incredible potential but how much of it do you actually use? If you are like most of us, only a small proportion. We are all capable of learning huge amounts of information. All we need are the skills. There is a wealth of skills that are so simple and available to all of us but because we've never been taught these skills, we don't use them.

Researchers are finding how to tap into more and more of our abilities, and we will experience big changes in the way information is taught in the next few years. We must make a habit of using these skills for our lives to be enriched for the benefit of ourselves and others

# My Areas of Expertise

This book does not represent the be all and end all of learning. Rather it is a collection of ideas which I have found to work. Since I intend you to use the book as a spring board, I am not going into any area in depth. Otherwise this book would be more like an encyclopaedia! I encourage you to take from the book as much as you can, then read further or seek out the professionals in the area. For example: the foods we eat have a bearing on our mental ability, and Rosemary Stanton has written excellent books to give this area more depth and authority. Anthony Robbins delves into goals, personal power, motivation and self-fulfilment. Svantesson will draw you further into the intricacies of mind mapping and memory. You will all follow your own particular interests, and be attracted to the information you need most. You'll be amazed how once these ideas are raised, your awareness of them will mean that you'll come across more information about them. And do, please, be critical. Question what I write about. You might for example feel the information about zinc is too good to be true, so ask your doctor or naturopath. Learning is a lifelong journey.

# Your Whole Body

There are many ideas in this book which will work for you. Some will work for you from the moment you apply them in your life. But to get the best results you really need to take a holistic approach. When your mind, body and spirit are in harmony, your growth and development will surprise you. When people join the army, for example, not only are they taught how to use weapons, they learn how good soldiers:

- walk
- talk
- eat
- breathe
- think
- exercise
- look
- sit

In other words it is a total approach taking into account every area of their being. When they master the interrelated skills in

all of these areas, they can be so much more effective. Perhaps we can learn something from the army. If you want to gain as much *Learning Wealth* as possible then let these ideas be in balance. Recognise that **the total you** needs to be involved.

# Summary

The following sections will show you some of the basic steps to tap your *Learning Wealth*. They are in alphabetical order to help you remember them.

| | | |
|---|---|---|
| a | affirmations | what are you saying to yourself? |
| b | beliefs | what you believe becomes your reality |
| c | colour | colour has power |
| d | delight | have fun learning |
| e | eyes | strengthen and co-ordinate |
| f | food | foods affect mental ability |
| g | goals | what you aim for is what you get |
| h | holistic learning | see, hear, be |
| i | integration | putting it all together, balance |
| j | justification | check out the successes |
| k | kinesiology | switch on your brain |
| l | listening | two ears and one mouth—use in that ratio |
| m | mind maps | whole brain thinking |
| n | NLP | senses and learning |
| o | oxygen | feed the brain oxygen |
| p | posture | move like a winner |
| q | questions | ask the right questions |
| r | reading | faster reading with better understanding |
| s | shorthand | new efficiencies in making notes |
| t | time management | time is your most precious resource |
| u | uppers | brain boosters |
| v | visualisations | believing is seeing |
| w | water | brain juice, drink of champions |
| x | excitement | get passionate |
| y | you | you in balance |
| z | zinc | zinc to think |

# How to Use the Book

Most of us are too busy to read a book from beginning to end unless perhaps it's a novel. I suggest that you start at the summary on the previous page and choose those topics which seem to be of the most interest or value to you. This probably means that they contain information which you consciously or unconsciously know that you need to deal with right now. Later, you can choose other topics in the same way. So this is an 'as you need it', 'pick it up' and 'put it down' type of book.

Highlight anything which strikes you as being of particular value. In fact, get yourself a collection of highlighters and use them liberally with the book. Use stars. Use coloured dots. Use anything, in fact, which will draw your attention to specific points. I have purposefully left wide margins so the book is easier to read AND so that you can put in your own marks and comments. This is your book. You have invested the money, so make it work for you.

Once you understand these ideas it is essential that you **put them into action within 24 hours**. Otherwise, they just become good ideas that you soon forget.

## *I hear and I forget*
## *I see and I remember*
## *I do and I understand.*

**Chinese Proverb**

# Why You Need to Put These Ideas into Action Straight Away (and keep at it!)

Only 10% of you will read past the first chapter and 90% of the information you read in this book will be **lost** from your memory **within 72 hours—unless...**

- <u>you</u> make a <u>commitment</u> within 48 hours to recognise the ideas that are meaningful to you
- <u>you</u> then <u>implement</u> the ideas within 72 hours

There are three levels to memory. The key for you is to take information to the third level.

## 1. Sensory register

This is the first level where your senses register information. You can only hold information at this level for a short period of time. For example, have you ever gone to the Royal Easter Show and seen thousands of faces? Could you remember them all now? No, because your sensory register rejected all that information very quickly.

## 2. Short-term memory

At this level information is held momentarily. You use short-term memory when you look up a phone number. If we don't transfer the information to our long-term memory, the information is lost. So we can hold information at this level for maybe a few minutes.

## 3 Long-term memory

At this level information is stored for long periods of time. *How old are you?* is a question requiring your long-term memory. It is important how we put information into our long-term memory so that we can get it back when we need it. This book will show you how you can firmly lock information into place in your long-term memory.

Can you understand now why it is important to do the exercises and implement the ideas? If you really want to put this information into your brain for your long-term use and benefit, then the information must go through these three levels.

Reading by itself will at best take you only to level two.

So the **Do It Now** sections at the end of each chapter are **vital** to develop your *Learning Wealth.*

> *Things do not change: we change.*
> Henry David Thoreau

---

### Do It Now

Your first task is to get some coloured textas, highlighters or pens to use in the book. And stars and dots too, if you want.

Go on, get them now or at least put them on your shopping list. The next idea might be the very one you want to highlight.

---

The **Do It Now** tasks are simple and if you use them, they are going to make the difference between doing what you've always done or beginning to build your *Learning Wealth.*

22

# AFFIRMATIONS

An affirmation is something we say, think or feel about ourselves which we believe to be true.

## Self-Talk

What you say to yourself determines how well you will perform. Your 'self-talk' is one of the most important factors in your success or failure at any task. I saw examples of this repeatedly when I taught speed reading.

At the beginning of each course, I had to assess students and find their baseline reading ability so that we could measure their progress. 'I want you to do a reading test', I would announce. The reactions followed a predictable pattern. Some would groan. Some would smile and sit up eagerly, keen to start. Some would look apprehensive. Then I always followed up by asking them to think about their instinctive reactions—to listen to themselves. How would you react? What do you think the good reader would say? What did the poor readers say? And were they right?

Some of the typical self-talk from good readers was: **'that's**

OK', 'this will be fun', 'let's go' and from the poor readers came self-talk like 'Oh no, I'm going to fail', 'I feel sick', 'this is going to be terrible'. How do you think this self-talk would prepare—or affirm—each of the students as competent readers?

We seldom take the time to consciously listen to ourselves, yet we are constantly chattering to ourselves. This chatter programs us for success or failure. You can edit and control this self-talk to turn it into positive affirmations. As my mother used to say 'You have the choice to see the doughnut or the hole in the middle, you choose to notice if the glass is half full or half empty.' Optimism is a learned habit and is essential for success (Seligman, 1990).

# Negative Chatter

Do you have any negative chatter or affirmations about your ability to learn well?

Many 'slow' learners have had a lot dumped on them.

> 'You'll never be any good at maths.'
> 'Great at sport—terrible in reading.'
> 'It doesn't matter. You can't have both beauty and brains.'

Stephanie Burns calls these *Great Lies We Live By* and has devoted a book to that title. Can you remember being told these lies as a child? Such lies are still with you, affecting your self-image. It's time to change these bad memories into something positive. If you have any bad memories then change them! 'But,' I hear you asking, '**how can I change memories of things that have already happened?**'

Once, I would have asked that same question. Then I had an experience which brought home to me the extent to which we can shape the world to suit ourselves. After my parents died my brother and sisters and I got together to relive and remember the past. I was amazed that we each believed and remembered such totally different interpretations of the same events. And yet for each of us our memories were very real. The point is that we chose to remember those things that fitted in with our view of the world and our affirmations.

If you have negative affirmations it is possible for you to change or reframe them into something more positive. Everything that happens to us is a learning experience. We can choose to remember **the learning** and this will **empower** us. Or we can choose to remember the **negative emotion** and this will **limit us.**

## Exercise in reversing negative chatter

In this exercise, the aim is to relive an event as it was, but to keep in mind the whole time the positive learning outcomes that could flow from it.

1. Choose a minor event that happened in the last year or so that left you with a negative emotion.

2. Now go back in your mind to 15 minutes before the event.

3. Imagine that you could have learnt something positive from the event. What would that be? Perhaps if you had an argument with someone you might realise that anger doesn't help. So think of something positive that you could have learnt even though this might be difficult for you to do. Right—got it now?

4. Now run the 'video' of the event in your mind, but see it as reinforcing that positive thought for you. The idea is not to rewrite history, but create a new interpretation of it.

## Now how do you feel about it?

If you were able to let go of the negative emotions and concentrate on the learnings then you're probably feeling pretty good.

The process we have just been using is called reframing. Reframing your memories into empowering learning experiences will help you to reshape your life and achieve your potential. Many of us are carrying frightening or deeply disturbing memories. If you are in this situation don't try to deal with this by yourself. Seek professional help. Time Line therapists use techniques similar to the ones we've just been using. They have the training and resources to help you deal with the more serious problems, if you feel you're ready to.

**There are no mistakes in life, only feedback.**

## Exercise: Putting your affirmations on paper

'I am a hopeless reader' is an example of a negative affirmation that could leave you feeling bad, frustrated and dumb. The positive affirmation from this could be '**My reading is getting better every day**' and then your response would be confidence.

**Now it's your turn**
Write one of your negative affirmations.

_____

What is your response to this?

_____

Write a positive affirmation to replace it.

_____

Now how do you feel?

_____

## Exercise with a tape recorder

Make a list of the positive affirmations that will empower you and record them. To fill up one side of the cassette you will need to go over the list a number of times. Let the tape play as you go to sleep so that you effortlessly reprogram your brain with more empowering self-talk.

There are tapes available of general affirmations which you could use if you find it difficult to make your own. But as soon as possible you should make your own, because the affirmations you choose will be the ones you particularly need. What's more,

27

if the affirmations are in your own voice your subconscious will tend to believe them all the more readily.

*Whatever you say to yourself today, you will be tomorrow.*

## Do It Now

1. Go to the mirror.
2. Look yourself straight in the eye.
3. Say aloud one of your new affirmations five times.

(Don't read on until you do it—I'm watching you!)

# BELIEF

How, you might wonder, are you going to believe in yourself when you are just starting out? Can't you only really believe in yourself when you feel, see and hear yourself achieving what you want to achieve? You've got a point. There's a simple answer. Actors have known for years if you haven't achieved it yet, you can fake it! Just as actors can fool an audience, you can fool your subconscious.

Researchers have found that whilst our subconscious mind is so powerful in so many ways it can easily be fooled. You've probably heard stories about Australian Aborigines 'pointing the bone' at someone. The victim dies, even though they might have previously been in perfect health. Why? Because the person believed they would die. Another great example is that of Mahatma Ghandi, who sincerely believed that India was for the Indians. For a long time, people thought that it was quite impossible to dislodge the colonial superpower, England. Ghandi proved them wrong. It took a long time, and Ghandi faced many difficulties, but in the end he was able to bring it about.

It's like magic. If you show your subconscious mind what it is

you are after in life, your subconscious mind will work for you to bring it about. When you apply your **subconscious** mind, your **conscious** mind and **all your abilities** to the task you become much more powerful.

I personally witnessed the power of the subconscious mind a few years ago when I went to a motivational seminar. I knew that one of the features of the program was a 4 metre firewalk. A couple of strong childhood memories made me rather nervous: as a 10-year-old, I was perched on a stool drying my hair when I overbalanced and almost rolled head first into the fire. You can understand why I was not keen on doing the firewalk. I didn't think I could walk on red hot coals—I didn't *want* to walk on red hot coals! However, during the seminar it was pointed out that the firewalk was really a metaphor about taking our fears and beliefs and by overcoming them, using them to empower us rather than to limit us. By the end of the evening, I believed I could.

I **knew** I would be able to do it, I could **see** myself doing it, I could **hear** myself being congratulated when I'd done it.

So I did the firewalk. It was an incredible experience. I knew then that there was even more that I could achieve in my life. Other people there amazed me just as much as the changes in myself: the young man of 18 who walked with crutches because one leg was at least 20cm shorter than the other; the woman in her 70s who was bent over and walked with the aid of a walking stick. Both of these (and just about all of the other 1500 people) walked across the bed of coals. I couldn't help but

wonder: **what else did they believe was possible about their lives now?** We were all able to do the firewalk because we **believed** we could, we were in the **right state of mind** and we were given the **skills.**

Remember, firewalks are a metaphor that worked for me. You don't have to do one to achieve the benefits of this book. In fact

I would advise you not to do a firewalk unless you can be sure it has been set up by a competent person and is absolutely safe. The challenge is not so much the firewalk but your belief system.

Suppose you believe you could never be wealthy. And yet when you look around at the people who are wealthy, you see that they are no brighter or more capable than you. At this point, you might have an unresolved problem. You could choose to wallow in self-pity, to believe that the rich must have been dishonest to accumulate so much wealth. Or you could decide to believe that if you began to do the same things that the wealthy have done, then you too could begin to be wealthy.

Which set of beliefs are most likely to increase your fullness of life? If this point seems particularly relevant to you then Robert Kiyosaki has written a great book called *If You Want to be Rich and Happy Don't Go to School* which you might you like to read as follow up

*If you believe you can or if you believe you can't, you're right.*
                                                            Henry Ford

### Exercise: What are the 'firewalks' that you need to accomplish in your life?

Let's say that my 'firewalk' is that I would like to sing in public. My proof would be to get a small part in a local theatrical production.

List eight things you would like to have in your life but don't believe are possible. To get you started I have completed the first one.

1.   Sing in public.

2.   _____

3.   _____

4.   _____

5.   _____

6.   _____

7.   _____

8.   _____

Now for each of these limiting beliefs what is the 'firewalk' experience or proof you need to show yourself that you're wrong?

What would it take to prove that you could do it? Look at the previous list and now write the **proof** for each one.

1.  Take on a small singing part in the local pantomime.

2.

_____

3.

_____

4.

_____

5.

_____

6.

_____

7.

_____

8.

_____

Beliefs determine your potential. Beliefs can turn you on to incredible energy and creativity or they can shut you down. When we believe we can do something, we often see a picture of it in our mind's eye. But what if we deliberately chose the pictures, rather than just letting them come to us? If we imagined a picture of something that hasn't even happened yet, something we **really** desire, might not our unconscious mind set about achieving it? The more empowering your picture and beliefs are, the more of your potential you will be able to realise.

## Visualisation exercise: Giving your brain something to model

These pictures which we deliberately develop to help us are called **visualisations**. As we now know, our subconscious mind is all powerful, but paradoxically is easily fooled. So this means that the process I am going to suggest is:

1. **Choose** a goal for yourself.

2. <u>**Imagine**</u> you have achieved this goal. What would it be like? I have a goal to play a piece of music perfectly on my violin. I haven't achieved this yet so I **imagine** I have. I create the picture in my mind. How was I standing? How fast did I play? How did I vary the loudness? And so on.

3. Now, **take your goal** and run the scene through in your mind like a videotape. Of course it's a fake, but it's a fake that helps us towards achieving the real thing: **fake it till you make it.**

All top performers set up their brain and their body to achieve the goals they have set for themselves. Good sportspeople such as golfers, tennis players, swimmers and runners mentally rehearse each move **perfectly** <u>**before**</u> they do it. Musicians and actors imagine themselves, on stage, performing **perfectly** <u>**before**</u> they actually go on. So, you too need to rehearse what it is you want. Do a perfect rehearsal so your brain knows what to do in the real situation.

Visualisations work best if they are repeated often. Some people are already using this technique unconsciously. Have you ever wanted a new car so much that you found yourself dreaming about it, imagined yourself driving it, pictured yourself parking it in the garage or heard the sound of its motor?

## Fun visualisation exercise

I haven't told you what this exercise is about because this would spoil it!
**Caveat: Don't do this exercise if you have any serious back problems.**

1.  Stand with your legs slightly apart.

2.  With one hand point straight in front of you.

3.  Keep your feet still.

4.  Turn and see how far you can twist around while still pointing.

5.  Make a mental note of that point.

6.  Untwist.

7.  Keep standing in the same position with your hands by your sides.

8.  Imagine that you are doing that exercise again. This time

imagine that even though your feet are standing firm you can twist your upper torso all the way round, back to that original position.

9. In your mind see yourself doing that again **at least five times** and each time turning all the way round.

10. Open your eyes and do it again for real.

**How much further can you go?**

---

### Do It Now

Picture yourself actually having achieved one of your goals.

Go on, close your eyes, take a break and **do it NOW**.

---

*You will see it when you believe it!*

**Dr Wayne Dyer**

# COLOUR

## How Can Colours Shortcut the Learning Process?

You can use colour to increase your productivity and the quality of your work. Because colour has the power to arouse your emotions, you can use colour to be more:

- **energetic**
- **creative**
- **receptive**
- **calm**

Throughout the long process of evolution, humans have had to use their eyes effectively. We are descended from fruit eaters, and all those years ago it was important to be able to tell if a piece of fruit was ripe without having to climb the tree. Colour was the key. Colour, we now know, is the key to much more than knowing whether fruit is ready to eat.

As John Miner in *The Complete Colour Reference Manual* points out, many of the major American corporations have spent millions on research into the psychology and impact of colour.

They are aware that colour has a great effect on our subconscious. An American airline company, for example, was stunned to find out that a change in their colour scheme aboard their planes had an immediate impact on profits. Originally, they had brown seats with red patches in the middle. After a change to more soothing green and blue pastels, their ticket sales picked up considerably. Research showed browns and reds in that enclosed environment made people feel nauseated. So, be aware of what colours can do to your subconscious and the subconscious of others.

Most fast food franchises for example are aware that:

- **Red** stimulates the appetite.
- **White** makes the red look stronger.
- **Yellow** attracts the eye and in small amounts stimulates the nerves.
- **Orange** causes people to eat and run.

Have you ever eaten in a restaurant decorated in shades of blue? For most people blue is an appetite suppressant, so you won't see blue in the successful food franchises.

Sometimes colour has effects which are quite different from what was intended. A few years ago I was setting up a new business and was looking at developing some corporate stationery. I spent a lot of time designing the logo and finally got everything printed on my favourite coloured paper—a pinkish grey. I was feeling very proud of this new expensive stationery and so I took it with me when I went to a colour course. We were asked to bring along anything that we needed colour advice on. It was my turn for 'show and tell' so I produced my new business cards and letterheads.

'This is my new corporate stationery,' I ventured, feeling all eyes were upon me.

One of the group hesitatingly commented, 'Oh, it's ah... very nice Roz'.

I could tell by the way she spoke that there was something amiss.

I thought I would bite the bullet and ask the obvious, 'You don't like it?'

John, a colour co-ordinator with a well-known paint company didn't beat around the bush, 'Well, it doesn't turn me on.'

I could sense by the way the others nodded in agreement, that his comments were supported by the rest of the group.

I was really proud of the stationery so I had to know more. 'What do you mean?'

Then Pam, a real estate agent in a bright red suit replied, 'Well it reminds me of ..... well, ... of a high-class ....... mortician!'

Horrors! I saw myself as a good communicator, so I wanted people to warm to me not be turned dead cold! Evidently I had chosen colours that I felt comfortable with rather than looking at the way others would react to them.

The brain loves colour. Anything that uses colour for emphasis will have more chance of being remembered. Most of what we read is black print on white paper. The monotony of these two colours makes it hard to remember the content. Occasional splashes of colour make information much easier to remember. You must have noticed how a colour page in a newspaper stands out?

# How Can You Make Colour Work for You?

Colours are a great way to turn your brain on. They act as quick ways to sort information.

Start colour coding information with that set of highlighters you purchased. Devise a colour code that means something to you. For example, you could use pink to signify problem areas or areas that need more research. You could use green to identify the ideas you are going to put into action straight away. Yellow could signify areas that involve others' assistance, and so on. I know some good teachers who refuse to use red in marking students' assignments. They use green instead, as it is not so threatening and doesn't arouse negative emotions.

You could develop your own colour coding. The following is a useful code for business professionals:

- **RED** items need an **urgent** response.

- **YELLOW** are **priority** items.

- **BLUE** items are to be **delegated.**

- **GREEN** items will go into a **report,** essay or project and so on.

You could try using different coloured paper to take down information. White gets so boring. Experiment!

## Colour exercise

Read through the exercise before you do it.

Sit quietly, breathe deeply and close your eyes.

Imagine that you have a lid on your head. Open the lid and start pouring white light in. Imagine that white light filling up your body, starting with your toes and rising all the way to your head. When you are 'full', let the lid close and be aware of how you're feeling, filled to the brim with white light. Bathe in the white light for a minute or so.

Now imagine that you have a plug in your heel. Picture yourself pulling the plug so all the white light runs out.

Replace the plug, open the lid and pour in a strong red. Let it fill you up as the white light did before, and then become aware of the effect of this strong red.

How are you feeling? What are you seeing? What vibrations are you picking up? Stay with the red for a minute or so and be totally aware of your response. Then let the red drain away. Pour the white light in again to cleanse you.

Next open the lid and pour a brilliant blue in. Let it completely take over your body and then allow yourself time to fully appreciate your response to blue. How are you feeling? What effect is it having?

Repeat the process with white light to cleanse your body. Take a few minutes to jot down the effect.

**White light**

_____

_____

_____

**Red light**

_____

_____

**Blue light**

_____

_____

And you didn't actually see the colour, you only pretended! Some people I have worked with have incredibly strong reactions with this exercise. How about you?

## Do It Now

Decide your colour coding for highlighters and make sure you always have a set on your desk. This book won't work unless you stop and take action **NOW**.

## COLOURS COMMUNICATE.

# DELIGHT

Take delight in learning. Have fun and pleasure undertaking the exercises. The more fun you have, the better you will remember the information. When you are relaxed and happy your ability to absorb information is greatly enhanced.

Human beings are playful creatures. Many of us have allowed playfulness to dwindle from our lives. Glasser in *Control Theory*, Grinder in *Righting the Educational Conveyor Belt* and many other researchers believe that being delighted and having fun is a critical trait of healthy, whole people. They also believe that we learn best when we're having fun.

> *Doing what you like is Freedom.*
> *Liking what you do is Happiness.*
> **Henry David Thoreau**

Schools are also coming round to the idea that learning should be fun. The progressive principal of my daughters' school has created an environment where all students are encouraged to learn and participate in activities. But, where this school differs from many is that students are also expected to 'enjoy their studies and have fun'. I know that my younger daughter Bella

felt a big boost to her confidence when she heard that phrase, as it was the first time that she had been given permission and encouraged to have fun at school.

The *Reader's Digest* have known for years the value of humour. Their regular section on Laughter, the Best Medicine is avidly read by millions all over the world, in a variety of languages. Doctors are also learning about the benefits of keeping their patients happy.

**Laughter is good for us because it:**

- raises endorphins (the body's happy chemicals)
- decreases cortisol (the body's response to stress) and helps us to relax
- activates the creative centres of the brain so that we show:
    - a tolerance for novelty, ambiguity and change
    - an increase in divergent thinking
    - an improvement in creative problem solving
    - a greater willingness to take risks

Seligman, in *Learned Optimism,* points out that **optimists:**

- achieve better results in their studies
- catch fewer infections
- have better health habits than pessimists
- have more effective immune systems
- live longer than pessimists

## Do It Now

This is probably the easiest challenge I've given you in the book. Think of your favourite joke and say it over in your mind. My motive is that you'll associate your joke with reading this book and you'll smile whenever you think of it. Remember a time when you had a good belly laugh.

# EYES

Using your eyes effectively will help them become stronger, and you will be able to read with much less fatigue.

Over the years the lifestyle of humans has changed. This is reflected in the way we use our eyes. Long ago we used our powers of vision to search the environment. We were always adjusting our focus from near to far with our eyes darting in many directions. These days we've moved away from this active visual searching to passive staring, usually at close range. Many of us use our eyes to stare at the one visual distance. We use computers for prolonged periods, or watch television for hours on end. This means eye strain and blurred vision. Our eyes don't get the chance to use their full range of motion and therefore the muscles weaken.

## The Eye is More Than a Camera

The eye has been likened to a camera, but it is much more than this. The eyes were formed in the embryo as two 'buds' from the brain. It is this *connection with the brain* which gives us sight, because the brain decodes the images seen by the eyes. The eye has a set of muscles, nerves and optical components which converts light rays into nerve impulses which the **brain interprets as vision.** So, the comparison with a camera is too simplistic because it doesn't take account of the developmental changes which occur. Gesell in his studies of children and their vision said that sight could not be considered in isolation. Vision involves the whole person.

According to Gesell **vision** was a system made up of:

- **posture**
- **manual skills**
- **co-ordination**
- **intelligence**
- **personality**

With appropriate exercises you can:

- **redevelop the full range of motion**
- **work for longer without eye strain**
- **delay the effects of ageing**
- **strengthen the muscles**
- **have healthier eyes**
- **regain more of your powerful sense of sight**

**Improving your sight is more than a physical task of wearing glasses.**

# Strengthen Your Eyes

About four years ago I was having trouble threading needles. I used to have to hold the needle so far away from my eyes that I couldn't see the hole. My children joked about how they had to thread them for me. At about this time I had been working with a developmental optometrist, looking at the relationship between eye muscle strength and reading ability and was impressed with the results. So I decided to overcome my failing eye sight and to strengthen my eye muscles in general. Using Janet Goodrich's book *Natural Vision Improvement*, I devised a series of exercises which I initially performed at least three times each day for two weeks. Now, I need to perform them only every couple of weeks, or whenever I feel my eyes need to sharpen their focus—and I have no trouble threading needles! Here are some of the exercises I found useful.

## Eye exercises

Always prepare for the exercises by relaxing yourself first. It's best to sit or stand comfortably with good posture, then relax and take five deep breaths. Rotate your shoulders then gently roll and stretch your neck. If you do the following sets three times a day for two weeks you should see and feel the difference.

1. **Shift your focus from a far away point to close up**
   Look at something as far away as you can, (maybe the top of a tree) then hold one finger in front of your eyes (20–30 cm). Look to the tree then to your finger and back again. Do this about five times. Then cup your hands over

your eyes and look into this cupped darkness for about five seconds. Looking into the darkness allows your eyes to relax.

2. **Move your eyes diagonally up to the left then down to the right**

   Keeping your head still, move your eyes as far up to the left as you can then move them down to the right and then back again. Do this five times then look into the cupped darkness of your hands for five seconds. Repeat the exercise, but this time look up to the right and down to the left five times, then look into the cupped darkness of your hands for five seconds.

3. **Come into and out of focus**

   Hold up a finger in front of you and look at a small mark on the top of your finger. Slowly bring your finger towards your eyes until you lose focus. Then slowly bring your eye into and out of focus. Do this five times and then look into the cupped darkness of your hands. (This exercise really helped me in getting out the children's splinters!)

4. **Close your eyes and turn your head to the sun**

   Close your eyes and turn your head to the sun. Look at the sun with our eyes closed for five seconds (it's dangerous to have them open!). Then turn your head away and look into the cupped darkness of your hands for five seconds. Repeat the exercise five times.

### Pinhole glasses

I found 'pinhole glasses' to be useful in improving my vision. I used them while I read a book or watched TV. These are not real glasses. They are made of black plastic, and instead of a lens, the plastic has pin holes. These holes cut down the light reaching the back of the eye and help to reduce blur. It's a bit like squinting when you're in the sun, but using the glasses doesn't tense the facial muscles.

I bought the glasses from the local health food shop and found that wearing them for about 30 minutes a day helped my eyes to relax. If you try them, make sure you don't wear them when driving, or at night, as they cut out peripheral vision.

The exercises weren't hard, but they helped me regain control of my eyes. My eyes can focus better at close range and they don't tire as easily. The exercises are helping me to achieve my objective of doing without glasses for as long as possible.

# Using Your Brain to Help Your Eyes

Vision happens when the brain interprets the images formed in the eyes. The next stage in your development is to improve the co-operation between brain and eyes. The exercises work in a number of ways. They make the eye muscles stronger and more flexible and they also get the brain to help the eyes.

### Eye and brain exercise

Here's a simple exercise for your eyes and brain.

1. Look all around the room.
2. Now close your eyes and think about anything you saw that was red.
3. No cheating! You have got to do it without opening your eyes.
4. Now look around the room and look for anything that is red.

When you looked the second time your brain was primed to take note of anything that was red. It follows then that preparation is the key to eye–brain efficiency.

**What you focus on is what you see.**

I remember when I was first pregnant. I couldn't get over the number of women in Bathurst, where I lived, who were pregnant. Had everyone decided to get pregnant the same time as me? I doubt it! Rather, in my scheme of things, being pregnant had now become a focus for my attention. Have you ever bought a new car and then been amazed how many there were of the same model on the road?

---

## Do It Now

It's about time you took a break.

Stand up.

Rotate your shoulders.

Look up as far as you can then look down as far as you can.

Do this five times.

Now look into the cupped darkness of your hands for five seconds.

You must do this exercise **NOW**.

---

# FOOD

## You Are What You Eat

Just as we say that a chain is only as strong as its weakest link, so too, you are only as healthy as your weakest cell. The cell is the smallest link in your body. How do you nourish your cells? Are you fuelling your body with high-grade fuel or is it contaminated with low-grade pollutants? Proper food and nutrition will help you learn smarter not harder.

### Sluggish lunches

In the full-day training programs I run, I now request that participants have a light lunch of, say, sandwiches and fruit. I have found that those who enjoy particularly heavy meals of fish and chips or pizzas tend to be very drowsy in the afternoon. Those who eat lightly are far more attentive. Participants who eat heavy meals use most of their blood supply and energy for digestion, rather than for learning. Whenever you are learning, fill your stomach only with easily digested foods so that it will support you rather than hinder your learning. Give your stomach 30 minutes or so after eating before you attempt any learning tasks.

## Sugar

In the years to come I believe that sugar will be recognised for what it really is. Refined sugar is a drug of addiction. It is not a food. It has no food value, only empty calories. It can dramatically alter brain chemistry and is highly addictive for many people.

Sugar has also been implicated in a number of problems such as:

1.  obesity
2.  mood disorders

3.   psychopathology
4.   poor development
5.   low IQ
6.   limited concentration span
7.   hyperactivity

If you want something sweet then fruit is the best source because the sugar in fruit (fructose) comes with vitamins and minerals.

## Water-rich foods

Your diet should be helping your body to cleanse itself rather than slowing it down with indigestible food stuff. When waste products build up in the body disease is likely. You can help your body to keep the bloodstream as free as possible from wastes and toxic poisons by:

1. Limiting the foods that strain your body, e.g., high fat and high sugar.
2. Providing enough water to help dilute and eliminate wastes.
3. Eating more fruit and vegetables and less animal products.

Elephants, gorillas and rhinoceroses are the biggest and most powerful animals. They are vegetarian and eat foods with a high water content. Humans are essentially vegetarians, who should limit their meat intake.

## Do It Now

Decide which piece of fruit you'll have for your next snack. Replace one red meat meal this week with a vegetarian or white flesh meal.

# GOALS

If you know what you want to achieve in life then you have taken the first step towards success. Successful people know what they want to be and what they need to accomplish. Goals keep your direction clearly in front of you; they let you know **when you've arrived** or if you are off track.

## Writing a Book

For some years I had thought about writing this book. Last year, I committed the goal to paper. I wrote down my goal and put an **achieve by** date on it: 'Write a book by Christmas and publish it by February'.

Writing down the goal focussed my thoughts and since we get what we focus on ...

A couple of months later I met two professional writers. These two started giving me the support and encouragement I needed to get moving on the project. Normally I wouldn't bump into professional writers even by accident. Writing down your goals is the first step towards making them reality. At first you might be startled at the 'coincidences' that pop up to move you towards your goal. As you write down more and more of your goals, you become accustomed to it. That's what happened with my book.

I started talking about the book in my training sessions. I was amazed and delighted when people started showing an interest in purchasing it. But I think the incident that really got me going was when a wonderful lady in Broken Hill wanted my autograph before I became famous!

Support started coming in from everywhere—even the most unlikely places! The initial desire to write the book became a pleasant obsession: 'I must get the book written...' And the rest, as they say, is history.

## Goals are Dreams with Dates on Them

Goals are essential if you want to start achieving anywhere near your potential. There is a saying that people who aim for nothing in life are not disappointed: nothing is exactly what they get! To succeed, you need to have a clear mental picture of what you want to achieve and an **obtain by** date. We need to write our goals in such a way that it seems they have already been accomplished.

There was a famous study done on Yale University graduates in 1953. The graduates were asked if they had clear, written goals including the steps for achieving them. Only 3% had their goals written down. In 1973, 20 years later, the graduates were studied again. The researchers found that the 3% had achieved more emotionally, socially and financially, than all of the other 97% put together. Naturally, the 3% seemed happier and more fulfilled!

# Setting Your Own Goals

The reason that setting goals achieves dramatic results is that success is all about knowing **exactly** what you want. This is a step that 97 out of 100 people **never** bother to take beyond their dreams.

Goals help you think clearly and make effective use of your time. It is little wonder that mature age students do so well at university. These students have a clear picture of where they are going and why. It is so much easier to work hard if you have a goal. Once you've set that goal, you need to have a burning desire to *achieve* it.

# S M A R T Goals

Goals need to be **SMART**       Specific
                                 Measurable
                                 Achievable
                                 Responsible
                                 Time related

## Specific goals

State exactly what you want *as if it has already happened*. Goals should be in the strongest, sharpest terms possible. Give them additional strength by stating them as if they were already a fact.

Instead of:  I want to do my Master's Degree one day.
Say:         I finished my Master's Degree by the time I was 40.

The more specific you are, the more the brain knows what to focus on and how to plan. The subconscious mind during sleep will also have something on which to work. You've probably seen the effectiveness of this yourself: you've racked your brains for a solution to a problem, then had the answer seemingly pop up 'out of nowhere' after sleep or some unrelated activity. Let the subconscious mind support you in your goals. Be specific and tell it exactly what you want.

## Measurable goals

How will you know that you have achieved your Master's Degree or whatever? Perhaps having a letter from the university congratulating you on your success and notifying you of graduation day.

Don't say:  I hope to pass my exams in December.

Say:        It is January 10th, I have received my results in the
            mail and have five A's.

## Achievable goals

The way to write goals is to set them up so that they are
achievable and **as though they have already happened** or in the
present tense.

Some people set goals in such a way that they fail. Suppose Sue,
a student, wanted to be a physiotherapist. She writes down
her goal. 'It is March 1996 and I have graduated as a
physiotherapist'. But already on some inner level she knows it's
not likely to happen—because she is very weak in maths and
science. Since she hasn't set complementary goals such as, 'I am
getting my grades up by 20% with an hour of maths and
science study every day', to remedy this situation, Sue has set
herself up for failure.

Some people actually set unachievable goals. Maybe it's a fear
of success that leads them to do this. So given the events in your
life and your commitments, you can determine which of your
goals are possible.

Instead of:  I'm going to work really hard. I'm going to study
             every spare minute.

Say:         Every weekday morning I'll get up at 5.30 and do
             two hours of study.

## Responsible goals

This means that your goals will benefit you and the world around you, they are ecologically sound.

Instead of: I hope to make time for my family.

Say: I set aside every Saturday afternoon from 1–4 to be with the family.

## Time related goals

When do you want them by? It's important to specify a 'have by' date otherwise all your time could be spent in planning rather than enjoying.

Instead of: I must use these ideas.

Say: Every Monday I will start working on a new idea from this book.

# WHAT ARE YOUR GOALS?

*Long-term*        **10 years from now**

List some of the things you would like to have, be or do, 10 years from now. Go for it!

_____

_____

_____

_____

**Five years from now**

What are some of the things you would like to have, be or do?
They might be steps to your 10-year goals or unrelated.

_____

_____

_____

_____

*Mid-term*          **One year from now**

_____

_____

_____

_____

**Six months from now**

_____

_____

_____

_____

**Three months from now**

_____

_____

_____

_____

*Short-term*          **One week from now**

_____

_____

_____

_____

## Do It Now

Write down your 10-year goal on a piece of cardboard. Put it where you can easily see it—perhaps on the bathroom mirror where you'll notice it every day.

Go on, **do it NOW.** This **really** is one of the most important exercises for your whole life.
Only read on if you've put the goal somewhere for you to see.

# HOLISTIC LEARNING

## How Can You Have Every Part of You Helping?

### We learn

1% *through* <u>taste</u>
1.5% *through* <u>touch</u>
3.5% *through* <u>smell</u>
11% *through* <u>hearing</u>
83% *through* <u>sight</u>

### We remember

10% *of what we* <u>read</u>
20% *of what we* <u>hear</u>
30% *of what we* <u>see</u>
50% *of what we* <u>see and hear</u>
80% *of what we* <u>say</u>
90% *of what we* <u>say as we act/do</u>

As you involve as many parts of you as possible in the learning process your ability to learn and remember increases. For example if you had to learn the road rules you could:

- read them
- write them down
- recite them
- get someone to test you verbally
- practise them in a car
- model a good driver
- rehearse mentally going for the test

## List 10 things you can do to make better use of all your senses.

1.

_____

2.

_____

3.

_____

4.

_____

5.

_____

6.

_____

7.

_____

8.

_____

9.

_____

10.

_____

## Do It Now

Choose one of those ideas and **do it now.**
Highlight it so that it will stand out.
Go on, put this book down and take action.
You must move from thinking to doing!

# INTEGRATE THE IDEAS

If you desire happiness, joy, ecstasy, love, or anything else then speak to yourself in terms of happiness, joy, ecstasy and love. What you desire strongly enough you will receive.

The ideas in this book are about you taking control of your life and using the power of your own thoughts, actions and beliefs to reclaim your strength.

Communicate with yourself in the most supportive way possible. Make every part of you as successful and integrated as can be—your:

- mind
  - body
    - spirit

When there is balance and growth in all of these areas then you truly move towards your full potential. Integrating the ideas and developing balance are the keys to *Learning Wealth* and personal fulfilment. How many times have you come across people who are so successful in one part of their life and a dismal failure in another? Just recently I met up with an old college friend who I thought 'had it all'. After a few minutes listening to the sad details of her disastrous marriage, and her husband's obsession with work and ambition, I realised how out of balance her life was.

# Exercise on Balance

### Mind...Body...Spirit
Write a goal for each of the above three areas in your life. A goal for your mind might be to read an inspiring book each month. A goal for your body might be to drink only two cups of coffee a day. A goal for your spirit might be to read some poetry, watch a sunrise, or go to church.

**Your turn**

**Mind**

_____

**Body**

_____

**Spirit**

_____

## Do It Now

Commit to one of the above goals now.

Write down the details of how you are going to accomplish it.

Do it **NOW**.

# JUSTIFICATION

The *Learning Wealth* ideas in this book are equally possible for all. And when you study successful people you will realise that they all embody many of the ideas presented here.

When **Arnold Schwarzenegger** was a scrawny youth living in Europe, he had a dream of living in the United States of America, becoming Mr Universe and then an actor. He believed it was possible, kept affirming his dream, supported it with visualisations, exercise and good nutrition. He read widely, studied effectively and had an absolute passion for his goal. Now Arnold, holder of the Mr Universe title, has starred in a number of popular films made in his adopted country, the United States of America.

**George Orwell** the author of *Animal Farm* was told:
    'It's impossible to sell animal stories in the USA.'
Since being published in 1945 *Animal Farm* has been extremely popular all over the world and was still being reprinted in 1987.

**Janet Goodrich**, the author of *Natural Vision Improvement*, wore thick glasses for 20 years. After using the eye exercises she writes about in her book, she was able to give them up. She also

had goals, and learnt the simple skills to achieve them. She now lectures all over the world on her empowering techniques.

**Colonel Sanders** was a retiree when he started out in business with a chicken recipe. He wanted to sell his recipe and was rejected 1009 times before someone finally accepted his idea.

**Chris Wilson** (not his real name), a Year 12 student, was floundering when I met him two years ago. His reading speed was 90 wpm (words per minute) and his comprehension was just 30%. Last time I tested him he was reading at 990 wpm with 90% comprehension. He was looking forward to finishing his HSC and going on to become a stockbroker.

You can do it too. There is no magic—just a determination to acquire the skills and do things a little differently.

---

## Do It Now

Choose someone you admire, who has many of the attributes of *Learning Wealth* which you desire for yourself.

Ask them the keys to their success. Don't be afraid to do this. Most people are flattered to think that you're interested.

Some will often help generously when you genuinely seek their help.

Name the person _____

When will you contact them?_____

---

# KINESIOLOGY...
# BRAIN POWER

## Here's how to switch on your learning potential

Brain researchers have found that though we possess a single brain it has two separate halves (hemispheres) which process information in very different ways. It's as if the average human had two brains, each with its own abilities and ways of solving problems. The two halves of the brain communicate with each other via a structure called the *corpus callosum*.

The two sides of the brain are involved in different learning processes.

| Left Brain | Right Brain |
|---|---|
| Logical/analytical | Integrated/holistic |
| Factual, logical | Whole picture/concept |
| Detail learning | Pictorial, musical, sequences |
| Convergent | Creative, divergent |

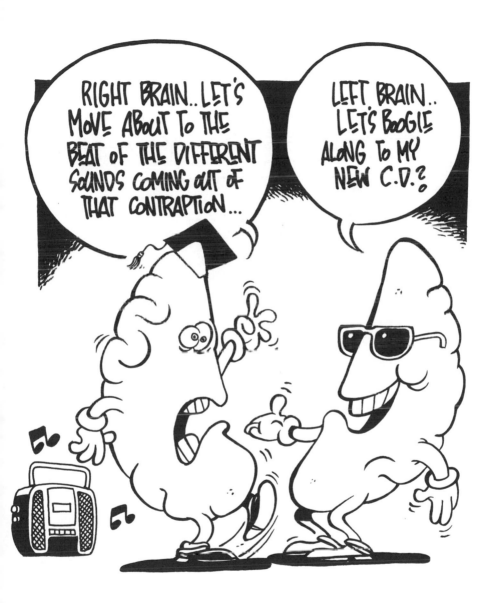

Our ability to learn is improved greatly when both hemispheres of the brain work in harmony. If someone has a learning problem it is often because these two halves are not communicating with each other. If you have better communication between the left and right halves of your brain you will learn and recall a far greater amount of information. You will learn smarter not harder. Kinesiology helps us first to **find** the blocks which keep us using only a small fraction of our brain potential, and then to release those blocks.

## Marching into school

When I was in primary school I was made to march into school. Left-right, left-right, once around the quadrangle and then into class. Those kids, who for one reason or another, didn't get the opportunity to march into the room tended to be scatty and usually had trouble learning to read. I realise now it wasn't just some militaristic dictator's thwarted sense of humour but rather a valid way to turn the brain on, although, at the time, I don't think the teachers realised the true value of the marching!

We have all heard the saying that you need to learn to crawl before you can walk. Crawling really highlights the co-operation of the two halves of the brain and body. Developmentally it is a great moment when a child moves using opposite arm and opposite leg rather than the two arms and legs together. The left-hand side of the brain controls the right-hand side of the body and the right-hand side of the brain controls the left-hand side of the body. Exercises like crawling and swimming require both sides of the brain to communicate

with each other. I know many remedial reading teachers who have their students crawling as part of their therapy. You can now probably make the connection between marching and integration of both sides of the brain: marching allows both sides of the brain to be stimulated and integrated.

Switching on the brain with these physical exercises is called **kinesiology**. Educational Kinesiology and Integrative Kinesiology have been around for well over 10 years. Although the empirical data is lacking in the area, the individual case studies are quite convincing.

## Switch on your brain

This is a great exercise to do if you have been sitting for over an hour and are feeling low on energy.

1. Start marching—you can either move around or on the spot.
   Come on now, lift those knees!
2. Keep your head still ... Really still!
3. Add figure-of-eight eye movements with your eyes.

This means look up to the right, down to the right then up to the left and down to the left and then up to the right and so on. This is called cross-pattern marching.

**This is a great energy booster.**

Here are some variations to really wake you up.

1. Keep doing steps 1, 2 and 3 above, now reverse the direction of the figure-of-eight.

2. March lifting the same arm and leg. This is called homolateral marching. Add the figure-of-eight with the eyes and also reverse the direction of the eye movement.

Crawling switches on the brain. You could do crawling too!

## · Do It Now

Take a two-minute break from this book.

Stand up and march on the spot. Come on, swing those arms and lift those knees!

Now, while marching keep your head still and rotate your eyes in a figure-of-eight motion.

Do not read on till you have done this exercise. This will make you feel more alert.

# LISTENING

Listening is one of the main ways we receive information. Regrettably, most of us are poor listeners and only use 25% of our capacity while we are working. We tend to think that we are good listeners but we can only give 100% of our capacity in short bursts, and only if the information is compelling. When we listen more effectively we can:

- reach a better understanding
- give appropriate responses
- have more effective communication
- be more productive
- improve our problem solving ability
- improve our relationships
- pay attention for longer

## How You Can Become a Better Listener

Listening well is an active skill. To do it properly, you must consciously want to improve. There is a big difference between *hearing* and *listening*. Hearing means that your ears have responded to the sound vibrations. Listening goes further, requiring you to have those sounds interpreted by the brain and then to give an appropriate response. I once read a story about the playwright David Williamson. His children used to approach him early on Sunday mornings when he was in bed and half asleep, with requests for money.

'Dad, can I have $10?'
'Huh, (mumble, mumble) here'.

The playwright heard what his children wanted but wasn't concentrating enough to really listen. His children knew perfectly well that they could obtain many things from their father as long as he was half asleep! If you'd like to follow this up, Hugh Mackay has written a very insightful book, *Why Don't People Listen?*, which has a more in-depth study of how to solve communication problems.

So to listen effectively we need to:

1. **hear information** ( How's your hearing? Do you need to get your ears checked?)
2. **select information from the speaker**
3. **attach meaning to the information**
4. **determine what we think about it**
5. **respond**

And all of this is done almost in an instant.

# Here are Some Ideas to Improve Your Listening:

1. **Pretend you have to pass on the information to someone else.** You will be amazed how much your listening will improve if you are listening in this way.

2. **Have a reason for listening.** Make the information relevant to you and look for ways you can apply it.

3. **Take notes.** If it's really worth remembering, jot down the key points. Put the information into a picture or mind map. (See the next chapter.)

4. **Be sure you make good eye contact.** If the speakers have something really interesting to say who are they going to communicate with most effectively? The person looking at them. A number of students have told me how making effective eye contact has helped them get on better with their teachers and led to improved grades.

5. **Ask and answer questions.** This helps to keep your brain active and also lets the speaker know if the message is coming across properly.

## Listening exercise

Spend the day in question mode. This means that if anyone talks to you answer back with a question. Strive to avoid dominating the conversation and encourage others to talk by asking questions. If they want information, you can answer their questions quickly and politely then re-adopt the position of a listener. You'll find it is a much more difficult skill than it seems. If you find yourself constantly talking rather than questioning, try again another day.

---

### Do It Now

For the next three hours when you're with someone only ask questions.

Unless you do this exercise straight away you will miss out on one of the key skills in listening. Do it **NOW**.

---

# MIND MAPPING

When you use both sides of your brain to learn, your potential increases dramatically (see the section on Kinesiology). **Mind maps** work because they are a whole brain learning technique. Most of our note-taking has probably occurred in a logical, linear and step-by-step fashion: a left brain approach. This is the way most of us were taught at school. When we combine this method with creativity, pictures, and getting the overview then we are using right brain skills. It is this combination of right brain and left brain which makes mind maps extremely powerful. The beauty of mind maps is that they allow you to maintain your focus while looking at the overview and detail simultaneously.

The value of mind mapping was brought home to me quite forcibly when I was on a committee trying to co-ordinate resources for people with disabilities. The meeting was leading nowhere. We knew it and couldn't understand why—after all, the members were making valid contributions. We just couldn't see where we were going.

Suddenly, as we discussed the issues, a picture of a wheel came to my mind, with the spokes representing the different interest

groups. I grabbed a piece of paper and started to sketch.

'What are you doing?' asked one of the women, breaking off what she was saying to stare at me.
'I've just had an idea,' I said. 'I'm drawing a picture of what this meeting represents.'
'Oh.' her forehead creased. 'It's a wheel.'
'Yeah,' said one of the others, peering over my shoulder as I labelled bits. 'And we're the spokes.'

'Yes.' I drew rough lines under the wheel, and added some quick circles. 'And these are the pot-holes on the rocky road, to represent the problems we've been having!'

The first woman took her own pen and reached around me to fill in one of the circles.

'Great. Now let's make this pot hole really big and black—this is our lack of funding,' she said.

Finally we could all see where we were going. It was like magic. This allowed the committee members to use their creativity and imagination to get back on track. We saw ourselves unified (as a wheel) turning together. Once we could get a picture or symbol of what we represented, then we could share the vision. The information was being represented in a whole brain rather than just a left mode.

*The idea is to create a picture of the information.*

# How do You Draw a Mind Map?

1. Get a large piece of paper—no less than A4 size. Turn it around as if you were going to paint a landscape rather than portrait. (Don't keep turning the paper around though, you must always be able to read what you have written.) Start in the middle of the paper with the main point or heading.

2.. Print the words and occasionally use CAPITALS for emphasis.

3. Use key words or trigger words—use words sparingly.

4.  Use textas and highlighters to add colour and emphasis. The brain loves colour.
5.  Use pictures and symbols rather than words.
6.  Make it unique. You'll love using these so make each one separate and easy to identify.
7.  Have fun and be creative. It doesn't have to be a Renoir. If it works—it works!

# Here is a Mind Map of this Chapter

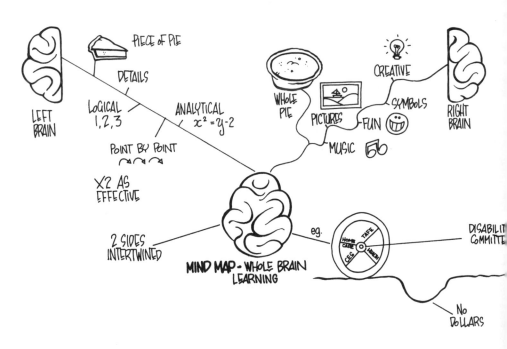

## Do It Now

Mind map key points that you have picked up from *Learning Wealth*. You must do it **NOW** or you'll never go any further with the idea. People often say to me, 'Good idea those mind maps', but I know they have no intention of using them. Yet, time and again, those who do make the effort to use them are amazed and delighted with the results.

99

# NEURO LINGUISTIC PROGRAMMING

To create our experience of the world we gather information through our five senses. Some of us use one particular sense more than others. 40% of us prefer to use our **visual** sense, 40% prefer the **auditory**. The other 20% experience their world mainly through a **feeling** or **kinesthetic** approach, and only a few learn through a **gustatory** (taste) or **olfactory** (smell) approach. Neuro Linguistic Programming (NLP) is the study of these different modes of focus or modalities. Knowing how we represent reality is important in understanding how to learn smarter.

If we make the effort to control the ways we represent the world to ourselves then we can develop:

- better ways of learning
- an awareness of the blinkered thinking in ourselves and others
- more effective communication

In the chapter on *Belief*, we realised the importance of self-talk. A knowledge of NLP will help us gain even more control over what we say to ourselves and others. For example, if I understand something which someone is telling me, my usual response is something like 'I <u>see</u> what you mean.' Someone else might say 'I <u>hear</u> what you're saying,' and yet another might reply 'Yes, I <u>grasp</u> what you're getting at.'

These are more than figures of speech. They are precise descriptions of the speaker's internal thinking. In each of these cases we have understood what was meant, but we chose a particular way to express our understanding. Bandler and Grinder in studying these 'figures of speech' discovered that these phrases indicate something fundamental about the way people perceive the world.

# How do You Filter the World?

### Exercise: Test yourself

I am going to give you a word and I want you to note whether your reaction is visual, auditory or kinesthetic. Are you ready? The word is:

## SUMMER

Did you get a **picture** of the brilliant sunshine in your mind?
Or could you **hear** the sounds of cicadas and birds?
Or did you **feel** the heat scorching your skin?
Perhaps it was the **smell** of bushfires or the **taste** of barbecued meat in your mouth.

Obviously we use all our senses but we have a preference for one. This is very important when it comes to handling new information. Suppose a report comes to you from your boss. Do you <u>see</u> all the implications? Or do you <u>hear</u> in your head your reactions to it? Or can you <u>feel</u> how it is going to be received? Maybe it leaves a nasty <u>taste</u> in your mouth or perhaps it's on the <u>nose!</u>

### How can you use this information to help you?

Work out what is your preferred representational system. Then make sure that you consciously use that mode to remember anything you want to learn or hear or feel (or taste or smell). Then try putting it into another representational system.

By the way, you are going well if you've read this far through the chapter. You'll really find the rest is easier to understand, so keep at it! This could well be the chapter that makes the difference to your *Learning Wealth*.

**Get the edge on others—be one step smarter.**

You can even work out the preferred strategies of others.

# Visual

Visual people tend to see the world in **pictures**. They use the visual part of their brain to represent reality. These people have many pictures racing through their heads so they tend to talk fast, trying to keep up with the pictures. They even use visual terminology. They say things like:

> It **looks** good to me.
> I **see** what you mean.
> I get the **picture.**

## Auditory

Auditory people take more care in the words they use and have more melodic voices. Words and the sounds of words are very important. Their breathing is deeper and more rhythmic. They tend to say things like:

> I can **hear** what you're saying.
> That **sounds** great.
> Yes, that **clicks.**
> That really is as clear as a **bell.**

## Kinesthetic

Kinesthetic people relate to feeling. They tend to talk slower, breathe deeper and use language from the physical world. They like to:

> Get a **handle** on things.
> Have a strong **grasp** of the idea.
> Be in **touch.**
> Get a **feel** for something.

We use all of the representational systems, but in a given situation we will have a preference for one above the others. Do

you see what I mean? Can you **hear** what I'm saying? Have you **grasped** this yet?

# Neuro Linguistic Programming— NLP

To return to my original point, NLP is about these visual, auditory and kinesthetic representational systems. It studies how the language we use affects our nervous system and therefore the way we perceive the world.

### Do you prefer auditory, visual or kinesthetic?

You will need a cassette recorder and egg timer for this exercise. If you haven't got an egg timer allow 1–3 minutes for each of the activities.

1.  Talk on to the cassette and without stopping describe all the things a visitor would **see** if they went to your house.

2.  Do the exercise again and describe all the things a visitor might **hear** if they went to your house.

3.  Do the exercise again and describe all the things that could be **touched** or **felt** or the **emotions** that you might pick up from the house.

When you do this exercise you'll find that one of the modes was easier and one was harder than the others. So do you prefer to learn by **seeing**, **hearing** or **doing**?

## Exercise on fun learning

Think back to a time when learning was really easy for you. When it was a pleasure to take in information painlessly and with joy in your heart. Think of a specific time. Perhaps it was when you were finally able to ride a two-wheeler bike. Maybe it was when you mastered the technique of driving a car, successfully completed an exam, or played a tune right through on the piano.

What was going on in your mind? What were you seeing at the time? What were you hearing, both externally and internally? That is, what were you saying to yourself? How were you feeling? Were there any particular tastes or smells associated with the learning?

Now that you know what you associate 'easy' learning with, you can start applying this to **anything** you need to learn.

Once you know which mode of representing the world is your favourite, you can start fine-tuning that mode to make it an even more powerful tool.

## Visual

If you prefer visual representation then get a clear picture in your head of a specific time or situation when learning was easy. Got it?

Is the picture a movie or still?
Is it in colour or black and white?
Is the picture right, left or centre?

Are you in the picture or watching from a distance?
Does the picture have a frame or is it panoramic?
Is it 2D or 3D?
Is there any particular colour?
Is the image bright or dull?

Once you've done this, begin to play around with the picture. See how you feel when you change the image. What happens, for example, if your image of being a good learner is a movie and you make it a still? Or being 'a good learner' is in colour, and you make it black and white?
Now experience the others.

## Auditory

If you prefer an auditory representational system then let's really hear what it was like when you were a great learner.

> Are you saying something to yourself or are others talking to you?
> What do you actually say or hear?
> Is it a loud sound or a soft sound?
> Is it fast or slow?
> What is the location of the sound?
> Is the sound sweet or discordant?
> Is there a regular rhythm to the sound or is it off-beat?
> Are there inflections up or down?
> Is there anything special about the sound?
> Did the sound last for a long or short time?

Now start playing around with the sound. If it was soft make it loud. If it was rhythmic make it off-beat. How do you feel about the changes in sound? Which changes empower you and which pull you down?

### Kinesthetic
If you are a kinesthetic person then how did you **feel** when learning was really easy for you?

> Were you hot or cold?
> Was there a rough or smooth texture?
> Was it rigid or flexible?
> Were there any vibrations?
> Was there an increase or decrease in pressure?
> Was there a change in relaxation or tension?
> Was there movement or direction?
> Was it heavy or light?
> Were feelings coming into your body or going out?
> Did it change size or shape?

Now start changing the characteristics. If it was hot make it cold. If there were no vibrations let it vibrate. If it was rigid let it be flexible. Go through all the dimensions and see which ones are powerful for you.

Make a note of the dimensions that empower you.

## Using NLP to Give You Confidence in Exams

Now let's say that some type of assessment is looming for you. Think back to the exercises that you've just done. Did you feel most confident in a visual, auditory or kinesthetic mode? Now use that mode and the aspects of it which gave you strength, e.g., colour, loudness or warmth to get into a very confident state. Deal with the examination while you are in that confident state. This process allows you to control your brain and to choose your emotional state.

# Using NLP to Remember Information

Now that you know a little about NLP and the way that you tend to experience the world it is possible to capitalise on that information. No matter which is your preferred mode you will learn and remember best if you use the techniques related to each of them.

# Visual Techniques

- read it
- look at it from every angle
- look for the big picture
- see the relationships with the various parts
- colour your notes
- turn the words into symbols and pictures

# Auditory Techniques

- talk about it
- hear it

- put it on tape and play it back
- read it out loud
- turn it into a song

# Kinesthetic Techniques

- write it down
- pretend you're part of it
- imagine the parts
- dance it
- turn it into a video in your mind
- put it into your dreams

---

### Do It Now

Choose something you want to learn from this book and list two ways from each of the visual, auditory and kinesthetic modes to reinforce the material.

---

# OXYGEN

When your brain has a good supply of oxygen, you think more clearly and work more productively. The brain is only 2% of the average body weight but it requires 20% of the available oxygen. Oxygen is an absolute essential for life and health. Every day we breathe approximately 11 300 litres of oxygen. We need all of this to keep the 75 trillion or so cells in our body healthy. Also, researchers have found that a lack of oxygen seems to play a key role in the development of cancerous cells.

The bottom line is that we are only as healthy as our smallest parts—so we are only as healthy as our cells. If you want healthy brain cells make sure that they are getting enough oxygen.

For 20 years of my life I was an asthmatic. My negative beliefs were that I **wasn't** breathing properly and that I **couldn't** breathe properly. I used to use a puffer to get air as deeply as I could into my lungs. I had to rely on a doctor's prescription to get access to the air which was freely available to everyone else.

I am no longer an asthmatic and one of the key reasons is that I now know how to breathe properly. Breathing controls the

amount of oxygen getting to each cell. And it is oxygen which stimulates the electrical processes of all cells. Also it is breathing which controls the flow of lymph fluid. This lymph fluid is sometimes referred to as the sewerage system of the body because of its critical role in removing wastes. You need to flush out the toxic wastes so that oxygen can effectively get to the cells. Breathing is essential then in stimulating the cells and removing the wastes.

# Breathe Deeply! Diaphragmatic Breathing

Deep breathing (or diaphragmatic breathing) works like a suction pump pulling lymph through the body. It accelerates the speed with which the body removes toxins.

# Not Hungry After Exercise?

Most people are not hungry after exercise because they are getting all the food/oxygen they need from exercising. Oxygen is the 'food' the body craves most.

### Breathing exercise 1:    Deep breathing
This exercise will make you aware of how you should be breathing. Lie on the floor with a book resting just below your navel. Watch the book rise as you breathe in, and fall as you breathe out. That's diaphragmatic breathing. It is the only way to breathe!

### Breathing exercise 2:    Removing wastes
This breathing exercise will help you to remove the toxic wastes from your body. Take 10 deep breaths three times a day breathing in the following ratio:

Inhale ... count of 1 ...  or 2
Hold  ... count of 4 ...  or 8
Exhale ... count of 2 ...  or 4

The air should be getting right down to your lower abdomen. If you have your fingers touching just below your navel, they should move apart as you breathe in and together as you exhale.

---

### Do It Now

Stand up and place your hands just below your navel.

Make sure they move out as you breathe in.

Take five slow deep breaths. You might be depriving yourself of precious oxygen so give your brain a boost and do it **NOW**.

---

# POSTURE

## Your Posture Affects Your Ability to Learn

How we move and hold our bodies determines, to a large extent, our effectiveness. For example, it is very hard to feel enthusiastic and alert when your head is drooping, your back is hunched, you have a frown on your face and you're yawning. Have you ever tried to learn in that position? But what happens to your mental state if you're leaning forward, eyes open, head up with face bright and alert? You will be far more effective!

**Your emotional state is created by how you hold and move your body.**

If you want to develop your *Learning Wealth* you have to be in the right emotional state and therefore the right posture. We even use terms of posture to describe emotional states. We say that people are rigid or inflexible Can you remember someone you've seen who was working effectively? What posture did they have?

115

# Don't Sit for More Than 30 Minutes at a Time

A straight spine allows oxygen and blood to move more effectively through your body and especially to your brain. Physiotherapists claim that sitting is the worst position to be in and that we should not stay in the one position for more that 30 minutes.

At 30-minute intervals we should get up and give our lower back a change of position, preferably by doing some simple exercises. If you've been leaning forward for a while, lean back, or vice versa. Listen to your body—often it knows what it needs. I'll bet many of you have stepped out of the car after a long car journey and immediately arched to give your back a complete change of position!

I first became conscious of the need to support my lower back when I was pregnant with our first daughter. I just could not find a comfortable sitting position, particularly at the dinner table. Then my husband and I realised that if we tilted the chair forward my spine would be straight and the pressure would be relieved. We put a block of wood under the back legs of the chair to raise it about 4 cm. This made an incredible difference to my comfort and alertness so I've kept the idea and routinely tilt my chairs. Sometimes I place a block of wood under the front of my desk to lift it, too, and this also makes for a much more comfortable working position. My students repeatedly report to me about how they like their tilted seats or tables and how much more productive they are.

---

### Do It Now

Make sure you have a comfortable chair that gives your lower back support. Roll up a small towel and place it so that your lower back gets even more support.

Push your chair right in to the table so that you are forced to sit up straight, and have the chair a little lower so that you are not leaning over. Go on, do it **NOW**.

---

# QUESTIONS

Over 60 000 thoughts go through our heads a day. Most are negative and most are the same thoughts as we had yesterday. What on earth are we programming into ourselves? Imagine how much more effective you would be if those thoughts were supporting you! Getting your brain to focus on the right questions will help you to concentrate, learn and remember.

How can you change these negative thoughts into empowering ones? You need to ask your brain to help you. Tell it what you want to find, and don't let random negative thoughts dominate your life.

## Turn Your Life Around with Questions

I have repeatedly stressed in the book the power of the subconscious mind, and you will find you can turn your life around if you ask the right questions. Your brain will help you if it knows what you want.

This is a critical insight for so many aspects of our everyday life. Just imagine being overweight. What will your brain do if you have that little voice in your head naggingly asking 'Why am I so fat?' Your brain being an obedient servant will answer of course. It will come up with some really unhelpful responses like:

You eat too much.
You're just like your mother.
You have no self-will.

Imagine what would happen if you changed the focus of your brain to empower you rather than belittle you. You could ask: **'How can I return to a healthy weight?'** Or **'How can I eat healthier food?'** Using questions every night before bed and immediately on waking will focus your mind on empowering thoughts. I have found this to really work for me. Some of my questions are:

> How can I be healthier?
> How can I be happier?
> How can I show my love for my family?
> What can I do to help others?

These questions then become the centre of my attention at a conscious and subconscious level and during the day I often surprise myself with the answers.

---

### Do It Now

Write down on a piece of card four questions on which you would like your mind to focus. Read them each night and morning for a week and watch how the answers appear.

Go on, do it **NOW**.

---

# READING

**In primary school you learn to read and after primary you read to learn!**

If the primary school system failed to teach you—it can be really tough!

We can all double or triple our reading speeds and improve our comprehension. Our brains easily handle 800 words per minute (wpm), but most Australians only read at 220 wpm with 60% comprehension. John F. Kennedy read at 5000 wpm and Jimmy Carter at 3000 wpm. And in one of the last classes I taught, a geologist read at 5950 wpm with 100% comprehension.

## YOU CAN DO IT TOO!

You can learn the skills to help you read at least twice as fast with better comprehension. When you break your bad habits and replace them with some simple skills you will be amazed how much more effectively you can read.

I spent every second year in primary school in the same class as

my younger sister. It was hell! She was academic and I couldn't read. Finally the school (it helps if your father is president of the P & C) put me onto a reading laboratory. On this program I did a little bit of reading every day at my own level. Later, I was dux of the primary school and owe my success to a system that worked.

Much later I did my Master's Degree and struggled through a mammoth amount of reading. I thought I knew how to read. But it wasn't till I finished my Master's and undertook a reading course that I really took off. I was so impressed with the course that I bought the franchise and started teaching the ideas myself.

## Breaking Bad Habits

The first thing with reading is to understand what slows you down.

**Saying the words to yourself one by one** is a habit from infant's school days. At first you were asked to read aloud so that the teacher knew what you were reading. Then you were asked to read quietly or read in your head. Some of you got into the habit of grouping words as we do in speech. Grouping words makes reading easy because words by themselves have no meaning. Grouping helps you read faster with better understanding doesn't it?

*Saying the words to yourself*
 *one by one*
is a habit
from infant's school days.
At first
you were asked to read
each word aloud
so that the teacher knew
what you were reading.
Then you were asked
to read quietly
or read in your head.
Some of you
got into the habit
of grouping words
as we do in speech.
Grouping words
makes reading easy
because words by themselves
have no meaning.
Grouping
helps you read faster
with better understanding
doesn't it?

A lot of us did not understand the importance of this step. If you keep reading quietly and say each word in your mouth (subvocalising) then you can only read as fast as you can talk. Normal speech is about 150 wpm. Race callers for example can speak at about 250 wpm but that is very difficult to sustain and is physically exhausting. So even if you read at 250 wpm and spoke each word you would find this difficult to maintain for more than a few minutes.

Subvocalising slows you down when you read. There are only a few occasions when you should consciously subvocalise:

- to help concentrate in a noisy setting
- to appreciate particularly well-written material
- to memorise specific information

## Exercise on saying the words to yourself

1. Have a lolly or some chewing gum in your mouth.
2. Reread the previous paragraph and if you can't read and chew at the same time then chances are you are still saying the words to yourself or subvocalising as you read.

Reading needs to happen in your head not your mouth.

You need to move from:

word → speech → brain

to:

groups of words → brain

and eventually to:

bigger concepts → brain

When authors write something they have a picture or concept in mind. They are never thinking 'what word can I say next?' Rather, they are thinking what is the next picture or concept to communicate. If you read each word at a time you will miss the bigger picture. So you need to get your brain tuned in to reading as well.

# How Can You Read Faster?

It can be difficult to break old habits. If you are a slow reader then you will want to spend a long time looking at each word and going back over it. So let's have some fun. This exercise will help you to move quickly from one word to another.

1. Choose a novel and turn the book **upside down.** (This way you won't mull over each word.)
2. Start in the top left-hand corner and use your index finger to point at the words and pace your eyes.
3. Move your finger evenly across the lines and make sure your eyes follow your finger.
4. Do this for a couple of paragraphs.
5. Go back to the beginning and repeat the exercise but this time even faster.
6. Repeat the exercise five more times and go faster and faster each time.
7. Turn the book right-side up and using your finger to pace yourself, read it again at a pretty fast pace. You didn't need to say each word, did you?

When you read words backwards and upside down it is almost impossible to gain any meaning from the text. So you disengaged that part of the brain which normally controls reading and used the eyes merely to look at nonsense groups of characters. With practice you can do this really fast. Then when you turned the page upright again and started reading, you probably realised how quickly you looked at nonsense characters. So why should it take so much longer to look at words when there is meaning?

If you are really keen to pick up your speed and comprehension then repeat the above exercise on a chapter of the novel rather than a paragraph. Your goal is to read in bigger groups or **chunks** of words so that you move from a:

        word
      ⌐ phrase
      ⌐ sentence
      ⌐ paragraph
      ⌐ page

Yes, some people can read a page at a time and the hardest thing for them is to turn the pages quickly enough. John Stuart Mill, the 19th-century genius once said that he couldn't turn the pages as fast as he could read them!

# Eye Movement Exercise

Our eyes do not move evenly across the page. The quicker and more effectively you move your eyes then, the more efficiently you can read.

You will need a partner for this exercise.

1. Sit facing each other.
2. You be person A and observe person B.
3. Person B is to keep their head still and look up to the left corner where the ceiling meets the wall.
4. Person B slowly moves their eyes following the line of the ceiling and wall to the other side of the room and back again.
5. Repeat the exercise and reverse positions.

What did you notice about the eyes? Did they roll smoothly like ball bearings, or were they jerky? Even when following a straight line the eyes jump around, moving forward and back, fixating on different points. This can be very distracting for poor readers. Poor readers, reading at less than 150 wpm, average more than 25 eye movements per line. No wonder their comprehension is poor: their eyes keep going back over what they have read, jumping all over the line.

From the exercise above most people's eye movements look like a pattern of funny Morse code. The eyes have stopped momentarily on the dots and for a longer time on the dashes. As well they jumped backwards and forwards. Their eye movements could well look like the example below.

. . _ . . . _ _ . _ _ _ . _ . . . _ . _ _ _ _ .

Instead you should aim for more even, definite eye movements from left to right without jumping back

You should aim    for three eye movements    per line.

_____    _____    _____

# Set Your Brain up for Reading

I've said that authors start with concepts or pictures and then put them into words for the reader. You, the reader, then take those words and create your version of the author's concepts or pictures. Wouldn't it be handy if you could get an idea of the big picture **before** you read? You can do this by **previewing.**

Just as you preview a movie, you can preview what you're reading. You skim over it quickly looking for the main idea; getting the big picture before you read in more detail. When I told you how to use this book in 'Getting Started', I suggested you first start at the summary and then go to those chapters that seem important to you. You will realise now that I was suggesting a form of **previewing.**

I often told my students that reading was like going on a journey to Yalwal. Chances are that you don't know where Yalwal is, so the trip may sound rather daunting and mysterious. If I give you the bigger picture and say that Yalwal is on the coast about four hours south of Sydney, do you have a better idea where it is now? And if I said that it was an old gold-mining town and that you turn off the highway about 30 minutes south of Nowra and then you travel along a dirt road for 20 minutes, would you have an even better understanding of the place? Well, previewing does the same thing. It gives you a general overview of where the author is taking you and it points out some key issues along the way. It doesn't take long to preview, but it really makes sure you are on the right track.

So you need to set up some questions which you automatically apply to everything you read to make sure you are on the same journey as the author. Here they are:

- **What's the main idea?**
- **What are the main points?**
- **How does the author support the points?**
- **How is this relevant to me?**

This last question, **'How is this relevant to me?'** is vital for comprehension and recall. Anything that you can make relevant to your own life, you will find easier to remember. Put yourself in the author's picture, and make what you're reading come alive.

## A Mop or a Debater

Read like a debater. Attack the material assertively: argue, agree or disagree, but have an opinion of it. Mops just soak up the information and fail to make it relevant. You need to make whatever you're reading relevant. Refuse to accept everything you see in print. Be sceptical.

## How to check your own reading speed

1. Get the average number of words in a line of print—count three lines.

2. Divide by three. Round down to the nearest whole number.

3. Count the number of lines you read in a minute.

4. Multiply this number by the average number of words per line to get your word per minute rate.

For example 10 words per line x 30 lines = 300 wpm

Do a reading course and read my next book *Reading Wealth*. A lot of what I've written in this section might make sense to you and a reading course might just be what you need to put more of these ideas into action.

### Do It Now

Reread this chapter and make sure you don't subvocalise. Have some fun! See if you can reread it and chew gum at the same time.

# SHORTHAND

Ten little words:

**a  and  I  in  is  it  of  the  that  to**

make up more than 20% of the written and spoken language.

Almost half of what we read is made up of less than fifty words.

Imagine how much quicker your note taking would be if you substituted an abbreviation or shorthand for each of them.

## Words as Symbols

If these words make up half the written language can you see how important it is for you to recognise them as symbols when you are reading? Just think of the symbols you already know like:

happiness

telephone

poison

You see and react to these automatically and you can react to the 49 words below in the same way. These are words that you have known and used since kindergarten. You really don't need to hear them in your head.

Here are the words with an appropriate shorthand. You'll need to practise these so that you can do it automatically. Don't worry, it won't take long, and you'll be delighted with the results. Here are the first 10:

| | |
|---|---|
| a | a |
| and | & |
| I | I |
| in | n |
| is | s |
| it | t |
| of | v |
| the | t |
| that | tt |
| to | 2 |

Here are the next 39:

| | | | | | |
|---|---|---|---|---|---|
| all | al | had | hd | so | s |
| an | n | have | hv | there | thr |
| are | r | he | h | they | thy |
| as | s | her | hr | this | ths |
| at | at | his | hs | was | ws |
| be | b | if | f | we | w |
| been | bn | me | m | were | wr |
| but | bt | my | m | which | wch |
| by | by | not | nt | will | wl |
| dear | dr | one | 1 | with | i |
| for | 4 | or | r | you | u |
| from | frm | she | sh | your | yr |
| has | hs | so | s | would | wd |

This version of abbreviations is a list of suggestions. You can add to these. Change them according to your own needs. In fact, the more you work in a particular area the more likely you are to have specialised abbreviations. I use **L** for learning and **R** for reading as these words come up frequently for me. Teachers, architects, lawyers etc. all have their own jargon which can be adapted easily to abbreviations. So, experiment! Find out which words you frequently use and create an abbreviation for them. The more fun you have with these, the more likely you are to use them and benefit from speedier note taking.

## Abbreviation exercise

The next two sentences will show you how easy it is to omit the vowels and still be able to pick up the meaning.

**If we omit many of the vowels we can make note taking quick and simple.**
**F w omt mny v t vwls w cn mk ntmkng qck & smpl.**

Because you are so familiar with the pattern of the English language you have no trouble filling in the_____ . You know my very next_____. So use this skill in your note taking. You have seen these words so often that you only need a few contextual cues.

**Yr eys & brn knw wt I'm wrtg! S lt thm hlp u. Tk t prssr ff. U dnt hv 2 c r hr evthg in dtl 2 knw wh s hpng.**

(Your eyes and brain know what I'm writing! So let them help you. Take the pressure off. You don't have to see or hear everything in detail to know what is happening.)

## Do It Now

Write the key points of this chapter in shorthand.

Wrt t ky pts v ths chptr n shthnd.

Go on, do it **NOW**.

# TIME

We all have 168 hours in the week. Some of us can achieve incredible amounts in that time and others do very little. How you manage time, and your attitude towards time, will determine how much you achieve. Many people's attitude towards time is held at an unconscious level and this determines the way they behave.

We spend time with the things we value. A wonderful example of this is that of a teenager and his new car. The young man lovingly spends hours cleaning it, admiring it, tuning it and repairing it. Older people while away whole days in their gardens. Why do they spend so much time nurturing these possessions? Because they love them.

Consciously and unconsciously, you spend time on the things that you value. And sometimes you are not really aware of how you divide your time. You may need to work out the priorities in your life, and apply self-discipline in managing your time. Many of us spend time dealing with the urgent demands on our time, and seldom devote enough time to the essential things. One of the key issues in time management is *how you distinguish between essential and urgent demands.*

*Things which matter most*
*must never be at the mercy of things which*
*matter least.*

**Goethe**

When I was doing my Master's Degree I thought I had my priorities all worked out. Getting assignments in on time I ranked as **essential** and **urgent**; spending time with my family I unconsciously downgraded to merely **important**. Later, when I studied time management, I realised that it was **important** for my assignment to be done on time and **essential** that I spend time with my family. **Essential** takes priority over **important** and **urgent**. Fortunately I could see that if I valued my family then they would have the highest priority.

Appreciating the distinction between **essential, urgent** and **important** makes all the difference to how successful you are in managing your time. The **important** activities can always be put off until tomorrow (and tomorrow never comes). The **essential** demands on your time get done straight away. So you need to look at what you value and put those values into priority order.

We all live with this constant tension between the **essential** and the **urgent.** If you spend some time analysing and planning your time you can learn how to make the best use of the time available to you.

# You Need to Know How You Spend Your Day

For example you could record on a piece of paper your activities each 15 minutes from when you wake up until bed time. This record will help you analyse what happens to you during the day. Then you need to analyse this information by answering the following questions.

**Where are the time wasters?**

_____

_____

_____

**When are you most efficient?**

_____

_____

_____

**How can you be more efficient?**

_____

_____

_____

**What can you delegate?**

_____

_____

_____

**What are the essential things you need to do ?**

_____

_____

_____

**What are the important things you need to do?**

_____

_____

_____

# Challenge

You would be amazed how much better you can use your time if you just spend 15 minutes a day planning. Time is our most valuable resource, but many of us just let it tick by. Each evening before you go to bed, list what you need to do the next day and then categorise those tasks as essential, important or low priority. Go to sleep with the knowledge of what needs to be done working in your unconscious mind. Then when you wake up in the morning read through the list before you start the day. This activity alone will you make you so much more focussed.

## 'NO' is the most powerful time saver in our society

Learn how to say 'no' in ways that don't offend. If you take on too much, your quality of life will suffer. You **do** have the right to say 'no'.

## Do It Now

Take a sheet of paper and write down your list of tasks for tomorrow. Then categorise them as:

I     important
E     essential
U     urgent
D     things you can delegate and so on

Now would also be a good time to start using your highlighters to colour code them in priority order, and use abbreviations.

# UPPERS

## Brain Boosters

If you have trouble getting started with study here are some ideas to give you energy. Or, if you feel jaded after studying for a while, stop for a few minutes and do a couple of these. Every 50 minutes at most you should stop and have a quick break. If you work for hours on end without a break your performance drops considerably.

Most of these are explained elsewhere in the book so this will be a summary:

- Drink a glass of purified water and have a glass on your desk so you can keep sipping.
- Jog on the spot for a minute or two.
- Have a picture in your mind of what you want to achieve next.
- Play some music that you find stimulating and supportive.
- Have a stretch, roll your shoulders, lean forwards, backwards, and to the side.
- Do some eye exercises.

- Breathe deeply. Take 10 deep breaths.
- Breathe using alternate nostrils.
- Massage your forehead with your index finger and thumb.
- Massage your ears.
- Take yourself to your perfect place (see *Visualisation*).
- Revise your affirmations.

## Do It Now

Do two items from the above list before you read on. You'll really find them refreshing! Do it **NOW!**

# VISUALISATIONS

When you have a clear image of what it is you want, then your mind can focus on it until it becomes reality. When you know you want *Learning Wealth* and you can see yourself achieving it, it can become reality. We have already discussed the power of *Affirmations* and *Beliefs* in earlier chapters, and suggested the power of visualisations. These three areas are intertwined.

Let's say, for example, that you are a slow reader with poor comprehension and you would like to be more competent. This is how visualisation would help.

1.   Sit quietly and relax.
2.   Breathe deeply and let your mind quieten.
3.   Listen to your breathing and allow yourself to enjoy the peace.
4.   Imagine yourself reading easily and quickly with excellent comprehension.
5.   Try to get a feeling in yourself that this mental image is possible.
6.   Experience the image as if it is already happening.
7.   Repeat this exercise two or three times a day.

You only need to have a belief that certain things are possible in order to use visualisations. So as long as you are open minded and have a desire to enrich your potential then visualisations will open up many possibilities.

I have a colleague who for years visualised himself teaching personal development courses in Russia. Now, 15 years ago most people thought his dream was impossible. After the Iron Curtain was removed he went to Russia and his visualisation became a reality. I wonder what he now thinks is possible in his life since he already has achieved the impossible?

# How do Visualisations Work?

When we carry out some action we always create it first as a thought or idea. 'I want to eat an orange' is the idea which precedes the eating of an orange. The mere fact that you are holding a thought or idea in your mind, is a like a magnet that will tend to create and attract the object of your desires. If you believe that you are a good learner, you become a good learner. This is more than positive thinking because it requires a much deeper commitment to changing our *Beliefs* and *Affirmations*.

Using visualisations helps you to choose and create more satisfying and enriching experiences.

> *You are a wonderful creative being*
> *living in a universe of wealth and riches.*
> *Be clear in your mind and heart what you desire*
> *and it will come to you.*
>
> Hazel Hughes

# Some People Don't See Things

Don't get hung up on the term 'visualise'. Some people get **feelings** for something or **think** about it. Our imagination is in constant use and whatever process you use to bring your imagination alive is OK.

> *...you are pure goodness;*
> *... everything within you is there to help you.*
> *When we baulk at experiencing our true feelings*
> *then we are limited.*
> *Be bold enough to experience life*
> *and its challenges to the full*
> *and you will be rewarded.*
>
> Hazel Hughes

# Visualisation Exercise of Your Perfect Place

In your mind you could have a picture of yourself being chased by crocodiles or you could have a picture of you relaxing on a sunny day by a river bank. This next exercise will show you how to get a picture of your perfect place so that you can gain access to it whenever you're in need of peace and harmony. It's best to read through the exercise first, then either read it onto a tape, or have a friend read it to you, or perhaps use the tape that goes with this book.

Get yourself in a comfortable position and start breathing slowly and really deeply.

Close your eyes and look up to the top of your head. (This helps to relax you).

In your mind take yourself to somewhere you know you can go to where you feel comfortable, safe and at peace with the world. It could be at home, in the garden, on a farm, by the creek or whatever.

From that place move along a pathway. This pathway is going to take you to your **perfect place**. A place of your own design and creation where everything is just perfect, just the way you would like it to be.

So in your perfect place how far can you see? Are you high on a cliff and can you see to the horizon? Or perhaps you are in a rainforest and can only see a few metres. And what does your perfect place look like? Is it in a cave, or a hut or perhaps you are floating on a cloud? Are there walls? Is there a ceiling? Where can you go to get into an extremely comfortable position? Is there a chair or a lounge?

What sounds can you hear are they loud or soft? What are you saying to yourself as you are feeling so comfortable in your perfect place?

How does your body feel? Is the temperature cool or warm? Is the humidity moist or dry? What are you wearing?

Now enjoy your perfect place where **everything** is just the way you want it to be. And as you're feeling so comfortable you'll see a video screen come on in front of you. It's going to show a movie of your life from now to many years on. Watch and enjoy the video because everything you see will be about you and the way your perfect life will unfold. Enjoy experiencing everything turning out perfectly—relationships, career, study, financial well-being, friends and family.

Then when you're ready, start becoming aware of your body and having a gentle stretch. When it suits you slowly bring your awareness back into the room. Take a few moments to reflect on where you've been and know that you have access to that perfect place and that video any time you want it.

---

### Do It Now

Think of something that you would like which is easily obtainable. It might be an object or event.

Adopt a comfortable position.

Start relaxing every part of you, starting at your toes and working up.

Slowly take 10 deep breaths.

Imagine the thing you want exactly as you would like it.

---

# WATER

Water is essential for the chemical processes of the brain, and this organ is one of the first areas of your body to react to a lack of water. Our body is made up of at least 80% water. Our planet is covered with 70% water. What do you think your ideal diet should contain? Yes, 70% water!

The best way to bring water into the body is through water-rich food (see F FOODS). 70% of the foods we eat should be high in water. But we know how busy people are—it's so easy to eat processed foods so if this is the case you need to be drinking far more water along with that food.

**Water, the drink of champions!**

Most of us live in a state of dehydration. This means we are not getting enough water. And one of the first parts of our body to show signs of dehydration is the *corpus calossum* which joins both hemispheres of our brain. Now our brain works best if both hemispheres are integrated and working together. If there is a lack of water in our brains, chances are that we won't be able to think and remember effectively.

When we drink too little, our blood becomes too concentrated. The poisonous waste products of tissue or cell breakdown are then excreted imperfectly. The body is poisoned by its own waste products.

If you had stud animals that had been working hard all day would you say 'Come on I'll get you a nice gin and tonic?' If they won a championship at the show, would you suggest celebrating with a bottle of champagne? I'm sure even on an ordinary day you wouldn't dream of offering them a nice white coffee with a couple of sugars. No, of course you wouldn't. **Water** is the only drink we give any animal that we truly respect and care for.

We need about two litres a day. Make sure the water you drink is the best—you don't want to add toxins to your body. Purified water has a delicious taste. The better the quality of water you drink, the more likely you are to want to drink it and make it a habit.

Lash out—try hot water; mineral water; water with a dash of lemon. Keep a glass on your desk. You will be amazed at how much you can and will want to drink if it's readily available.

Tea, coffee, alcohol and sugary drinks are diuretics. This means that they take even more water out of your body. Limit your intake of these, and increase your consumption of water.

We called water **RAIN JUICE** in our house to get the children more comfortable with drinking it. It worked too!

# Are You Drinking Enough?

The colour of your urine is a good check to see that you are drinking enough water. Your first wee of the day may be yellowish. All the others should be almost clear. If you find that they are bright yellow during the day, then you are not drinking enough water.

---

### Do It Now

This one is easy. Go and get yourself a glass of water. Always have a glass of water on your desk.

Go on, do it **NOW**.

---

# X-EXCITEMENT

People with *Learning Wealth* have an excitement and thirst for knowledge. It is this passion that many people seek and which propels them to great heights. When you get excited about what you're learning then your ability to understand and remember information will astound you.

It's excitement about an idea that keeps people up late at night and gets them out of bed early in the morning. It's excitement and passion that keep people hanging in long after others give up. It's excitement that we crave in our relationships. And when we have excitement our potential is just about limitless.

Get **excited** about what you're learning.

---

### Do It Now

Choose one chapter of this book that really turns you on and share what you've learnt with someone.

Which chapter?  _____

Who are you going tell? _____

Come on, do it **NOW**.

---

# YOU

## How Are You Going?

How are you handling all of this information? Are you pacing yourself so that you give yourself enough time to put each chapter into action before you move on? Remember that whole books have been written about each of these chapters, and I encourage you to go to the references to support and develop your *Learning Wealth*.

As we mentioned in the chapters on *Integration* and *Holistic Learning*, a balance is required. Be conscious of developing harmony in your own needs, the needs of your family and your work needs.

> *One ought*
> *every day at least,*
> *to hear a little song,*
> *read a good poem,*
> *see a fine picture,*
> *and if it were possible*
> *to speak a few reasonable words.*

**Goethe**

## Do It Now

Congratulations you have beaten the odds! You are one of the 10% of readers who have made it beyond the first chapter.

Reward yourself! List one nice thing you'd like to have as a reward for getting so far through the book. Perhaps you could buy or borrow another book, or take yourself out to lunch, or sit in the park.

**What's your reward?**

Write it down.

_____

Do it **NOW.**

# ZINC

Wouldn't it be wonderful if you could press a couple of buttons or pop a few pills and then everything you wanted to learn would be installed in your memory forever? Alas, it is not possible yet, but there are a number of simple things you can do to make you learn more efficiently.

'Isn't there just one pill I could pop to help me learn better?' you ask. Well, the answer is yes! I know. It's a bit hard to believe, isn't it?

One of my daughters is fairly active. I wouldn't actually say hyperactive, but when she was eight that description would have been apt. Fortunately, I had read and heard about the wonders of zinc, and here I was with a ready-made guinea pig. Bella was unsettled in class, very easily distracted—you probably know the type. So I quietly put her on a zinc tablet each day. Two weeks later the teacher said: 'What's happened to Bella? She seems so much more focussed in the classroom—more at ease somehow.' To me, it was obvious. The zinc had taken effect.

## So How Could Zinc Have Helped?

Zinc is essential to life in a number of ways. Over 2000 enzymes in the body need zinc to carry out their work. Smoking and repeated infections can lead to zinc deficiencies. A zinc deficiency may manifest in a number of ways such as the

159

loss of the sense of taste or smell, skin disorders, and slow wound healing.

1.  Zinc is vital for nerve and brain functioning.

2.  Zinc is essential for our bodies to grow and develop physically. Zinc plays a vital role in nutrition, and it is needed to metabolise carbohydrates, fats and proteins.

3.  Zinc is essential for the production of sperm and in male sexual development in particular. It is often recommended for male sexual problems. Zinc is also important at all stages of the reproduction process in women.

4.  Zinc is needed for the genetic material in DNA to form and function properly.

5.  Zinc has a vital role to play in the immune system.

6.  Zinc can help overcome the toxic influence of cadmium, mercury and lead.

Zinc has been found to be helpful in a number of mental disorders such as schizophrenia, anorexia and bulimia. It is no surprise that a loss of appetite is a symptom of low zinc levels.

White spots on the fingernails are often an indication of a zinc deficiency.

## Where can we eat our supply of zinc?

A number of factors have limited our zinc intake. Australia is an old continent and a lot of the zinc has already been leached from the soil. The craze for high fibre diets means that a lot of zinc is not absorbed. Lean red meat is a major source of zinc, but this is often one of the first foods to go when people diet.

Zinc is not a panacea for everything, but it does seem that it can be helpful in assisting mental processes. A bottle of zinc tablets can be bought from the supermarket relatively cheaply. If so many of us are zinc deficient due to our diet, stresses and toxins in our environment then a tablet a day could be a great investment. It's best to take the zinc tablet at night as absorption is highest then.

---

### Do It Now

Go and write zinc tablets on the shopping list. If you haven't got a list then start one.

Go on, do it **NOW.**

---

# CONCLUSION

Congratulations! You've made it to the end. You obviously have persistence, and that is one of the key qualities that you'll need as you develop your *Learning Wealth*. As I said before, only 10% of people who pick up a book read beyond the first chapter and so you are one in 10. You are indeed a rare and special person. Well done!

## Where to Now?

The best thing for you to do now is to start reading some of the books in the reference section. Of course by now, you're already incorporating many of the ideas from this book and experiencing great success. So keep having fun with them.

---

### Do It Now

Take your highlighter to the reference section and choose your next book to read. Make a note in your diary to borrow or purchase it. Do it **NOW**.

Thank you for allowing me to share my ideas with you. And enjoy achieving your *Learning Wealth*.

---

# REFERENCES

Agardy, F.              *How to Read Faster and Better*
                        Collins, Sydney, 1985.
Bandler, R.             *Using Your Brain for a Change*
                        Real People Press, 1985.
Bandler, R. & Grinder, J.
                        *Frogs into Princes*
                        Real People Press, 1979.
Bone, D.                *The Business of Listening*
                        Crisp Publications, California, 1988.
Burns, S.               *Great Lies We Live By*
                        Caminole, Sydney, 1993.
Collis, J.              *Yes You Can*
                        HarperCollins, Sydney, 1993.
Covey, S.               *The 7 Habits of Highly Effective People*
                        The Business Library, Information
                        Australia, 1990.
Dyer, W.                *You'll See It When You Believe It*
                        Morrow & Co, New York, 1990.
Edwards, P.             *Seven Keys to Successful Study*
                        ACER, Melbourne, 1989.
Gawain, S.              *Creative Visualisation*
                        Bantam Books, California, 1982.
Gesell, A. Ilg, F. & Bullis, G.
                        *Vision: Its Development in Infant and Child*
                        New York, Hefner, 1949, reprinted 1967.

Glasser, W.            *Reality Therapy*
                       Harper & Row, New York, 1975.
Glasser, W.            *Control Theory*
                       Harper & Row, Toronto, 1984.
Goodrich, J.           *Natural Vision Improvement*
                       Viking O'Neil, 1985.
Gore, A. & Tasker, D.
                       *Pause Gymnastics—Participants Handbook*
                       CCH, 1988.
Grinder, M.            *Righting the Educational Conveyor Belt*
                       Metamorphous, Oregon, 1991.
Haynes, M.             *Personal Time Management*
                       Crisp Publications, California, 1987.
Hendler, S.            *The Oxygen Breakthrough:*
                       *30 Days To An Illness-Free Life*
                       S. & W. Information Guides.
James, T. & Woodsmall, W.
                       *Time Line Therapy*
                       Meat, California, 1988.
Kehoe, J.              *Mind Power*
                       Zoetic, Vancouver, 1992.
Kiyosaki, R.           *If You Want to be Rich & Happy Don't Go to*
                       *School*
                       Excellerated Learning, California, 1991.
Mackay, H.             *Why Don't People Listen?*
                       Pan, Australia, 1994.
MacGregor, S.          *Piece of Mind*
                       C.A.L.M., Sydney, 1992.
McCarthy, B.           *The 4 Mat System*
                       Excel, Illinois, 1987
Miner, J.              *The Complete Colour Reference Manual*
                       J. Miner, Carina, Brisbane, 1990.

Parker, A. & Cutler-Stuart, M.
*Switch On Your Brain*
Hale & Ironmonger, 1986.

Pease, A. & Pease, B. *Memory Language*
Pease Learning Systems, 1992.

Peck, M. Scott *The Road Less Travelled*
Rider, London, 1987.

Robbins, A. *Unlimited Power*
Simon & Schuster, Great Britain, 1988.

Robbins, A. *Awaken the Giant Within*
Simon & Schuster, New York, 1992.

Rose, C. *Accelerated Learning*
Accelerated Learning Systems, Great
Britain, 1985.

Rusk, T. & Rusk, N. *Mind Traps*
Thorsons, California, 1988.

Seligman, M. *Learned Optimism*
Random House, Sydney, 1990.

Stanton, R. *Eating for Peak Performance*
Allen & Unwin, 1994.

Sun, D. & H. *Colour Your Life*
London, Piatkus, 1992.

Svantesson, I. *Mind Mapping and Memory*
Kagan Page, 1989.

Wade, J. *Super Study A New Age Study Guide*
Dellasta, Melbourne, 1991.

Wilde, S. *Affirmations*
White Dove, USA, 1987.

Williams, V. L. *Teaching for the Two-Sided Mind*
Touchstone, Simon & Schuster, NewYork,
1983.

# More Information About Developing Your Inner Wealth:

- Reading Wealth
- Learning Wealth
- Living Wealth
- Health Wealth
- Writing Wealth

You can continue to develop many aspects of your inner *Wealth* by reading more of the series or using tape programs. Roz Townsend offers a range of opportunities for you to continue acquiring the riches within.

If you are interested in taking these ideas into your organisation then Roz' skills as an exceptional speaker and trainer will have your staff laughing all the way to the top!

You can contact Roz by facsimile on:

063 314500 Australia

61 63 314500 International

# About the Author

Roz Townsend has had a wealth of experience teaching and training at all levels. Her most recent programs have involved training over 4000 people in speed reading, plain English, negotiating and study skills programs.

Roz has teaching experience from kindergarten through to TAFE and university lecturing. She has worked in many special needs schools and before setting up her own consultancy and training program Roz undertook postgraduate studies at the University of London and the University of New England. She was awarded a Bicentennial grant and Apple Foundation grant for her work with people with disabilities.

Showing people how to use and develop their own learning skills is Roz' great passion. Her radio interviews and public speaking engagements attract great interest and support. She is now a highly sought-after speaker showing people how to more effectively use their brains.

Learn the A–Z of Developing your *Learning Wealth* from one of the best in the business!